I0471795

50 MONSTER IDEAS TO GET

MORE

website links
& customers

© Alan O'Rourke
All rights reserved. No part of this book may be reproduced or transmitted in any form or by any means, electronic
or mechanical, including photocopying, recording, faxing, emailing, posting online or by any information storage
and retrieval system, without written permission from the Publisher.
All content and images copyright of the respective companies.
For more books, resources and guides visit http://audiencestack.com/static/books.html

Tactics

How to use this book

One of the core factors on how well your site ranks in Google search results is what other websites link to you. Google figures that if other people like your content so will the people using their search engine. But getting other sites to link to you is not so easy.

Contained within are 50 proven strategies used by websites across the world to get more links. These are Ideas you can try for your own website but for best results you should approach them systematically. Share this book with your team and pick out 10 strategies that you think would work for your website and with the resources you have.

Create a spread sheet and describe the idea. Set the same budget and time frame for all ideas so that you can compare results. Decide who is responsible for implementing the idea. And describe what you hope the expected results to be.

Example:

IDEA: Create an Infographic based on an existing report into successful sales teams. Promote the Infographic to all people who linked to the original report and to sales related websites.

TEAM: Joe and Designer

BUDGET: $500

TIME: 1 week. Infographic creation and outreach requesting a link/mention.

EXPECTED RESULTS: 20 new links.

Repeat the tactics you find that work and the another round of testing with the next 10 tactics from the book.

Enjoy.

Alan

50 Link Building Stratagies

1. Create a badge or award.

Select the top websites or blogs in your business niche or reward the top users on your own website. Rank them and issue an award for being the best. Then give each one an award badge to display on their site with a link back to your site. Of course if all the links back to your site are from the same award it can look unatural so use this tactic along with others here for variety. See point 5.

Lesson: Appeal to your users ego. Anything that makes them look great or tells others they are great will tend to be used.

2. Create a focus for your product with a National Day.

Wil Reynolds from SeerInteractive.com persuaded a client to give away $5,000 worth of products for a National Day they created especially for their niche. This campaign created a focus for discussion, PR and hype that resulted in so many links and traffic, that his client's website went down.

As an added bonus the company collected over 3,000 email subscribers and sold over $10,000 worth of products.

A non-branded mini website was created for the campaign which achieved links from four of their main competitors. Six months later the company redirected (301) the mini site to their main site, with all the links generated now pointing directly to them. This year their competitors are asking if they can be part of the national day promotion.

Lesson: Create a day for your product and do not be afraid to do it unbranded if you can get value from it later.

Create a badge or award.

3. A great idea without a plan is useless.

Your idea might be great, but if you have no clear step by step plan on how to promote it, then do not do it. "Build it and they will come" does not work. Paul Cawley from http://learninbound.com warns: "Don't forget that your time is limited and you need to treat it as a resource. If you're wasting time on unproductive tactics that don't help your strategy, that has a cost to you".

Lesson: Submitting to Reddit.com and Twitter.com etc. is not a plan.

4. Update old popular content.

Find pages 8-10 in Google search results for your target keywords. Pick out old, popular content with out of date information such as infographics, reports, how to guides etc. Update this information. If you can expand and improve upon it and post it on your own website. Using a tool like OpenSiteExplorer.com look for all the sites that link to the old content. Email each site and tell them the information has been updated and where they can find the new version with a link to your website.

Lesson: Build on other writers short attention spans. They started a blog and wrote great content but didn't stick at it to keep it updated.

5. Do not be too aggressive with your link building.

A particular website got too many sites to link to them with the one keyword phrase (Blue Widgets). So much so, that it began to look unnatural to Google. The client had 29% of their inbound links for (Blue Widgets) but their competitors only had 2.5% of inbound links with that same phrase. So instead, spread links more naturally across, 'Big Widgets', 'Red Widgets', 'How to use Widgets' etc. for more natural looking statistics.

Lesson: Unnatural looking inbound links can be penalised by search engines. Find out more about preventing link penalties here: http://backlinko.com/prevent-google-penalties

6. Build an army.

Do not wait until you need to promote something before you start connecting online and on social networks.
Build your network, social and email, before you need it to build trust and authority.
Retweeting and sharing other people is a good strategy to build connections. People will be more likely to share you when required.

Lesson: No point launching stuff if you have no muscle behind you to push it.

7. Give free content.

Want to get the top resource sites in your niche to link to you? Give away free content. Write a blog post, provide news or write a report. We take unused images and designs from our agency and post them to Flickr.com free for others to use in their blog posts. This has resulted in links back from high profile sites like Mashable.com and adweek. com

Lesson: Websites are crying out for quality content and like you, have very little time to produce it. Give it to them.

8. Make your app or content embeddable.

Rackspace.com the hosting company are a great example here. They made their web mail login form embeddable, just like a like a YouTube video. Users can copy a piece

free

$0

Give away content.

of code and put it on their own company website where staff can login and check their mail. Rackspace have a few form types with different Keywords in the link back. Again mix this tactic with others. See point 5.

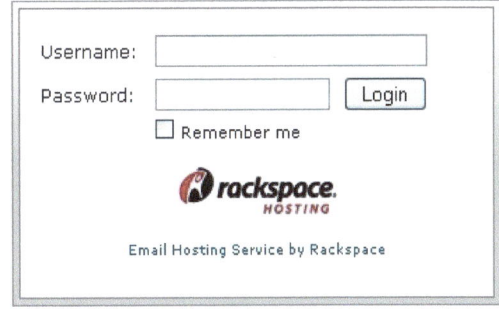

9. Sneaky idea: Incentivise embeds.

Pay (a few hundred dollars) to top bloggers to feature your infographic. The return is not the link you get back from them directly (it doesn't matter if they put a No Follow link on it) the result is from all the followers these top bloggers influence, who then reblog and share your infographic on their sites. So you pay once for many results.

"The tool https://klout.com/ can be a good way to find influencers for networks."

- Paul Savage from EmailTrainer.com

Lesson: Influencers matter.

10. Look for opportunities on Twitter.

Wil Reynolds set up a search for the phrase "lost my phone" on Twitter which returned thousands of results every day. Will then sent a tweet to each user with a link to a software programme that can help find the phone. Sometimes the link would contain a competition to win a new one. This simple campaign created lots of inbound links from people happy to see an opportunity to get a new phone.

Funny note: Will also set up a search for "Girlfriend stole my phone" but couldn't understand why there were such little results until he changed it to "B$%&# stole my phone".

Lesson: Know your audience and their language.

11. Never try to replicate someone else's backlink profile.

Be careful about copying what your competitor is doing as you could end up copying all their crappy, spammy links that can damage your ranking. First, create a market overview of all your competitors in a spreadsheet. Paul Cawley suggests tracking Position in Google results, Domain authority, Page Authority (from https://moz.com/), Linking root domains, Trust Flow and Citation Flow (from https://majestic.com/). Once you can see who is rising and falling in your industry, you can investigate why.

Lesson: Be sure you know what works before you copy it.

12. Don't waste time complaining about competitors.

Google does not like to see websites paying for links It views it as cheating the system and can and does devalue your search ranking. However if you see your competitor buying links it is not worth complaining to Google about it. It is hard to prove and takes up too much of your time.

"If it's not something that will move the needle for you, you shouldn't be wasting time on it. It's just costing you time and money." suggests Paul Cawley

Lesson: Focus on where you get the return.

13. Monitor links to competitors.

If you spot the competitors page now gives a 404 error (page not found) identify the content missing using the the wayback machine http://archive.org/web/. Try to rewrite and improve the content and republish on your own site. You can then follow up with everyone linking to the old page and ask them to link to your page instead. Some suggested email text to try

"Hey, I noticed this link on your site to a "blue widget guide" is broken. I found this other one that Alan wrote reciently if you want to fix the link to a guide that works".

14. Get listed on directories and press release websites.

Check the Search Engine Journal directories list at www.searchenginejournal.com/web-directories. Paul Cawley of LearnInbound.com explains some recent changes to this tactic. "Low quality directories and press release sites have been hit hard by recent algorithm changes like Panda and Penguin aimed at reducing low quailty link farms. However, if a site is highly moderated, contains high quality information and is edited to a high standard preventing spammy marketers from taking advantage there still are opportunities here. Hyper local directories and industry specific niches tend to add a lot of value for users and have a high barrier to entry, ensuring they stay valuable in the search engines and users eyes."

Lesson: Grab the low hanging fruit!

15. Revisit link sites.

After a couple of months, go back to your Reddit.com or Hacker News posts and ask all sites that linked to that post to change their links to the content on your website instead. Be prepared to pay $10-$20 for the hassle of changing the link.

"Some may ask for an administration fee to change the links, but most would be delighted to do it if you've added additional value or extra resources on your own site making it more valuable for their visitors." - Paul Cawley

16. Follow through on pages that link.

A link is not much good if Google does not see the link. When a website links to you, ping Google on that site's behalf to make sure the page it is picked up and indexed.

17. Don't be afraid to ask people to change links.

Find out who is linking to your social media posts or discussions in forums and ask them to link to the source material on your own website instead.

18. Or ask them to change how they link.

Find out who refers traffic to you and make sure they have an SEO friendly link. If they don't, ask them to change it.

19. Top tips on viral incubation.

You have 24 hours to drive your content to Viral Status. After this time it becomes exponentially harder.
- Encourage forum discussion
- Catch community action early

- Watch for organic inbound traffic from forums that you can incubate.
- Register on the forum but post in other discussions before moving to your own post.
- Regularly comment on the thread to keep it alive and near the top of the forum.

20. Ask for reviews.

This is a great idea from Brian Dean over at Backlinko.com. Search for blogs in your niche on Google that might be interested in what you sell. Reach out to them with a carefully worded email and offer it for free. Brian provides an example:

```
Hey (site owner name),

I was searching for some homepage soap recipes today when
I came across (site name).

Awesome stuff!

Actually, I just launched a guide that teaches people
how to make luxury soaps at home. I usually charge $X,
but I'd be more than happy to send it over to you on the
house. All I'd ask is that you'd consider mentioning it
on your blog or writing a review.

Let me know how that sounds.

Cheers,
Your name
```

He does warn not to violate Google's Webmaster Guidelines by making the review optional and not specifically asking for a link.

21. Help a reporter out.

This is one of my favorite tactics that I have been using for years. Helpareporter.com (HARO) is an email list where reporters say they are looking for experts on various topics. You get a daily digest of all these requests and if you spot a request for your industry simply reply and tell them how you can help. This can result in mentions and links from a wide range of publications, online and off. In my exprience I would get picked up for 1 in every 10 requests I reply to.

22. Widgets and plug-ins work.

Website are always looking for new content or features to make their website more useful. Create something that can be easily embedded on a website as simply as a YouTube video. But make sure the embed code has a link back to your website. Ideas: Calculator, video, infographic, form, survey, poll, data feed plug-in etc. Alternate the anchor text you use. See point 05.

23. Control your link text.

When you create widgets or plug-ins try and control the link text and URL via a central server. This way you can change back links in future across all sites. So with one change on your server you can move all the sites linking to site A linking to site B.

> *Lesson: Your business, product or keywords may change. Set up a way to change your inbound links at once.*

24. Language matters.

The language you use on your own website and marketing dictates how people describe your product / page when linking to it with anchor text. For example Moz.com changed the heading and link on their discussion forum web page from "Questions & Answers" to "SEO Q&A Forum" as they are the keywords people searched for. People now use those keywords when linking to the forum.

25. Does your content deserve to rank on its own?

Instead of trying to rank a series of individual posts on a topic look at creating a new portal page on the topic's subject with links to the individual posts. Link in and out to this page. Collectively it should rank higher and be worth sharing. Which leads us to...

26. Make use of old content and links on your website.

Example: You might have old posts from 5 years ago that is not very relevant any more and does not get many visits. Instead 301 redirect them to updated or more important pages.

27. Read the Excel Ninja Guide.

Check out the Distilled Excel Ninja Guide on how better to use excel in your SEO research. http://www.distilled.net/excel-for-seo/ As well as helping you organise your link building efforts it is a great example of giving away free content in return for links.

28. How many 5 year olds could you take in a fight?

Look at "How many 5 year olds could you take on a fight" quiz for a great example of link bait. http://www.buzzfeed.com/daves4/how-many-five-year-olds-can-you-take-in-a-fight
Lesson: Mad and funny always works. Challenging friends is even better.

29. Crowd source content.

Example: Ask your network on Twitter or Quora.com: "What are the best sites you would recommend for learning marketing?" Take the answers and write a blog post or report. The answers form a great resource on the best blogs people should read. Those blogs listed will probably link back to you. See also point 1.

"I'm a fan of google trends to see what and how people are searching." - Paul Savage

Lesson: EGO bait always works.

30. Outsource your link building.

There is a range of link building duties you can outsource including:
- Finding URLs, targets and filtering those results.
- Content creation.
- Measuring.

Lesson: Link building can be a big job but you do not need to do all the donkey work.

31. Avoid looking spammy.

When scaling your link requests avoid looking spammy by the following:
- When gathering targets filter by what type of links you can get.
- Write down and record a few notes about each site to personalise the email link request you send out.
- Mail merge to personalise the emails you send.
- Have a backup plan in case someone asks for a link back or for a guest post.

32. Have a great design.

Spend a little extra time getting the site design beautiful. You should be doing this anyway but an added bonus is, you can get your website featured in the hundreds of design showcase sites on the web. Search Google for [CSS HTML Showcase Gallery] and start submitting your site.

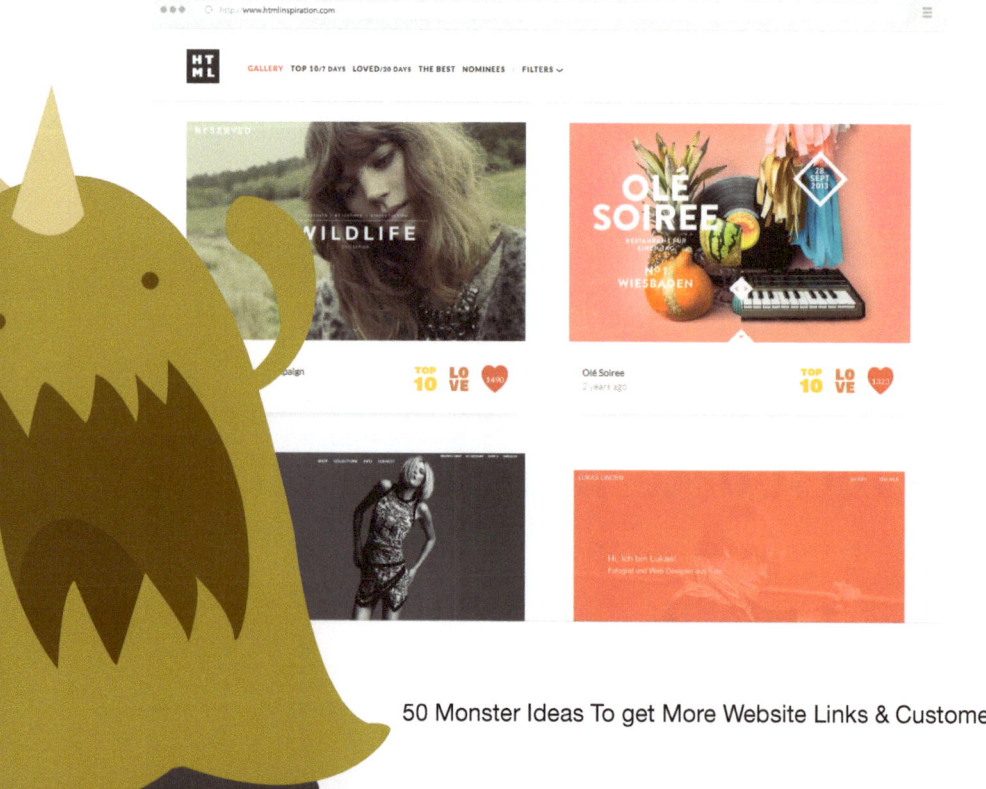

33. Spend time on the better targets.

Some sites and links are more valuable than others. Spend more time on the valuable ones to improve your chances of getting a link back.

34. Become a content resource in your niche.

One of the best examples I have seen of this is from Mark Brownlow who created the site www.emailisnotdead.com which compiles research and statistics on the email industry in the one place. Everyone in the email space refers and links to this page.

35. Find discussions to join and seed content.

BoardReader.com and BoardTracker.com can search and rank forum discussions for keywords or competitors. Become a member for a while, and contribute to discussions before you start pushing your own links.

36. Do High quality research.

Compile some research that will save others time and effort. Take a look at (search for) Oyster.com photo fakeouts. They researched photos from hotel brochures and websites and compared them with their own photos. The results very linkable.

37. Register your business everywhere.

Register your business and address across loads of sites on the web. See https://moz.com/local. It is important to keep the format of your name and address details consistant across these sites.

38. Find guest posting opportunities on Twitter.

Another great tip from Brian Dean. In Twitter search you can search for the keywords "Your Topic" + guest post.
Results from the last week show you sites that feature guest bloggers that you should approach and pitch your content. Variations of the keywords to search include:

"your niche" + guest post

"your niche" + guest author

"your niche" + write for us

"your niche" + guest article

39. File patents and/or fund scholarly research.

Want a link from the patent office? File a patent (slow). University? Fund some research (less slow). Paul Cawley goes on to suggest:

"If you have a local charity you can sponsor, not only can you gain from any backlinks earned but you also earn from the even greater benefits of helping the

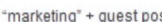 
"marketing" + guest post

Top | Live | Accounts | Photos | Videos | More options ⌄

Zach Heller @zheller · 3h
New **Post**: **Marketing** for the Masses (**Guest Post**): The following is a **guest post** by Lexie Lu. Lexie... bit.ly/2aJLC8O #zachheller

Marketing for the Masses (Guest Post)
The following is a guest post by Lexie Lu. Lexie is a designer and writer. She constantly researches trends in the web and graphic design industry. She writes weekly...
zachhellermarketing.com

BYU Museum of Art @BYUMOA · 3h
Guest blog **post** by our **Marketing** student: buff.ly/2aZtoRs
#byumoa #artrocks

  ♥ 1

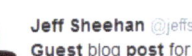

Jeff Sheehan @jeffsheehan · Aug 10
Guest blog **post** for @IBM: The Future of the Ecommerce Customer Journey #CX #**marketing** ibm.co/2bild3q lnkd.in/eVaWPi4

 5 4

Asian American Media @asianamericanm · Aug 10
Interested in contributing to @asianamericanm? Hit us up! #**guestpost** #business #**marketing** #socialmedia #media #strategy #wordpress #seo

♥ 17

FE International @FEIntl · Aug 9
Read Founder @ThomasSmale's **guest post** about 4 common #**marketingautomation** mistakes and how to avoid them

4 Common Marketing Automation Mista...
Discover the 4 mistakes people make...
automation and what you need to k...
digital marketing strategy for bu...
blog.getfocusedonmarketing.co...

local community and the trust that can bring". (Much faster!)

40. Build your social profiles.

Set up the following: Facebook company page, Google profile, Slideshare profile, Twitter profile, Crunchbase and AngelList page, Reddit account, Linkedin company page, Quora profile, Instagram account, YouTube account, About.me, Stackexchange and Github account, Pinterest profile, Tumblr, and Wikipedia profile.

41. Discover where big brands get their links and see if you can.

Use a tool like https://moz.com/researchtools/ose/ to find what sites are linking to a particular Domain and see if you can also get links there. But be careful and read point 11.

42. Create Twitter/Facebook/ Instagram/Reddit centric content.

Communities like to read and discuss topics about themselves. Think ego baiting on a bigger scale. So for example, if you do a post on the history of Twitter, people on Twitter are more likely to link, share and discuss your post. You can use tools like Moz.com/Followerwonk or BuzzSumo.com to help identify what content is working for others in a niche and see how that can be improved upon for even better results.

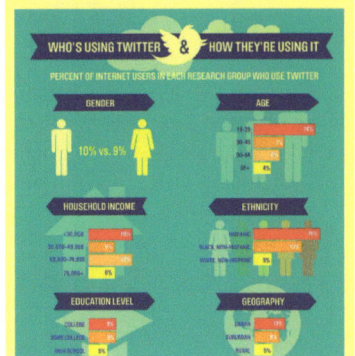

43. Find bloggers with lots of fans.

Use FollowerWonk or Klout to find bloggers with lots of followers and influence. Offer to do a guest post or provide other value to them or their readers which would result in a link back to your site.

44. Host/Sponsor/Attend events, Meet ups & conferences.

Look at lanyrd.com, Meetup.com or search for events on Google to find conferences you can sign up for and get listed online as an attendee.

45. Send someone a testimonial.

Send a testimonial to someone with your photo and link back to your website. Most people will put it on their own website because it makes them look good.

Lesson: Again EGO baiting always works.

46. Do a video.

Long tail of video sites get 50% of all online traffic/views! That's too much traffic to ignore. Start with creating a video version of some of your existing content. Put it online and let people share and embed it.

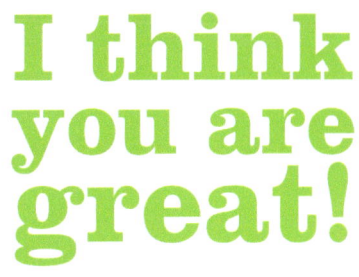

47. Create high quality infographics.

An infographic is a visual graphic showing various statistics on a topic or industry. It gives people an easy visual way to understand numbers and statistics. People love sharing and linking to them. Looking for infographic inspiration? Try searching on Pinterest.com

48. Get on key, industry reference listings & directories.

Lists of construction companies in New York, list of key blogs in the online marketing industry or designers in the London. Each industry has lists. Find yours and ask to get listed with a link back.

49. Tweets are a valuable link.

While Google might not use links on twitter as a ranking factor research has shown that links with a lot of shares get more links from other websites. Anything that improves your discoverability and makes more people aware of your great content means you have more chance of them linking back to you or sharing the content with even more people. So get people talking about you.

Lesson: Start talking to people on Twitter and give them a reason to share your links with their audience.

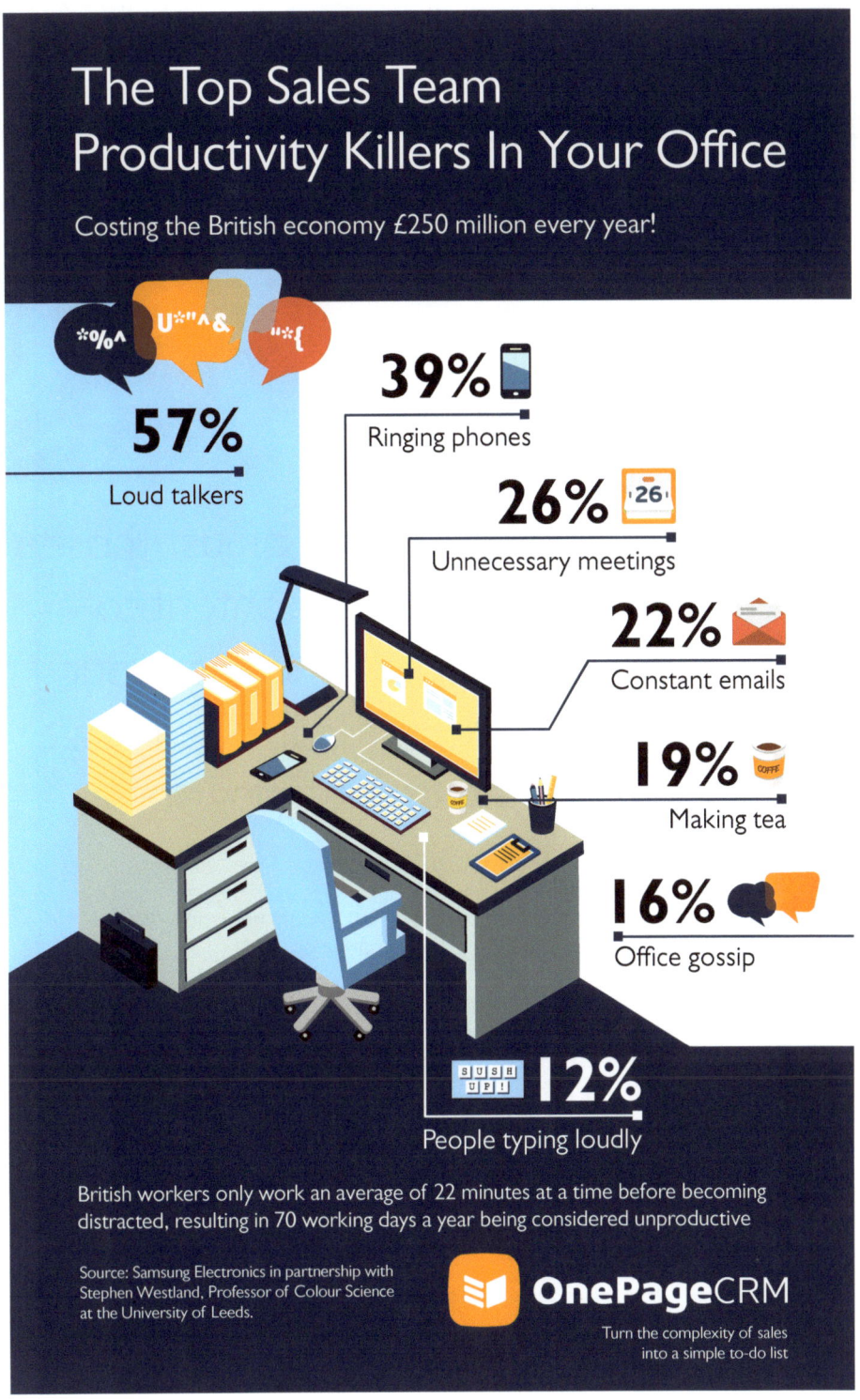

The Top Sales Team Productivity Killers In Your Office

Costing the British economy £250 million every year!

57% Loud talkers

39% Ringing phones

26% Unnecessary meetings

22% Constant emails

19% Making tea

16% Office gossip

12% People typing loudly

British workers only work an average of 22 minutes at a time before becoming distracted, resulting in 70 working days a year being considered unproductive

Source: Samsung Electronics in partnership with Stephen Westland, Professor of Colour Science at the University of Leeds.

OnePageCRM

Turn the complexity of sales into a simple to-do list

50. Pay for tweets or shares.

You do not have to wait for others to tweet about you as you can pay Twitter for promoted tweets which usually get retweeted if useful. According to Paul Cawley

"If you have identified the influencers within your niche (FollowerWonk), create a targeted Twitter list of just those power users. Promote your content to those and you dramatically increase your chances of them sharing it with their large following of targeted users, giving you a type of 'Paid Organic Boost'"

Larry Kim has some great advice for working with Influencers here: http://www.wordstream.com/blog/ws/2015/02/26/influencer-marketing

Note: These links are great outside indicators to Google that you are a trusted source of information. However inside make sure that your own website is set up correctly. Luckily Google will tell you anything you need to fix. Log in to https://www.google.com/webmasters/tools/ and set up your website. Then do anything Google tells you to do.

50 Monster Ideas To get More Website Links & Customers

About the authors

Alan describes himself as an ex artist, ex film maker, ex designer, ex product manager and ex entrepreneur. He is currently VP of Growth at OnePageCRM.com and author of a few marketing books. One of which you hold in your hands.

Alan was previously a creative director with over ten years of award winning creative strategy, marketing and user engagement design. Author and speaker, Alan previously ran one of Ireland's leading design agencies where he was nominated for a BAFTA award. Alan later founded online marketing software company Toddle. com, building a user base of almost 30,000 users worldwide before selling the company. He is a graduate of business development in DIT but more importantly studied film and he almost made it to the big time as an extra on TV's A Tale At bedtime with Podge and Rodge playing snooker player #2 but they didn't show his good left side.

 alan@spoiltchild.com

 Linkedin.com/in/spoiltchild

 @alanorourke

You can also follow Alan under the alias @ben_approves as he showcases some of the best email designs on www.beautiful-email-newsletters.com

He writes about sales and marketing at http://audiencestack.com

Mary Carty is an award winning entrepreneur with a background in art, education and startups. Working with leading international companies, cultural institutions, universities and non-profits over the past ten years; while building a startup and running an online agency, has taught Mary a few things about making it in an ever-connected world.

Creativity and curiosity are her twin passions. Mary's background has given her a unique insight into building and marketing companies, products and services. I

 mary@spoiltchild.com

 Linkedin.com/in/marycarty

 @marycarty

Photo credits

New York Times by B.K. Dewey
http://www.flickr.com/photos/
bdewey/3374674246/

Doughnut image by eskimo_jo
http://www.flickr.com/photos/eskimo_
jo/3970017189/

Point 6 Clone Troopers by myrrh.ahn
http://www.flickr.com/photos/
ahnmyrrh/3613617899/

Point 7 Concert Crowd by Anirudh Koul
http://www.flickr.com/photos/
anirudhkoul/2046282436/

Point 45 Twitter Stats by pewresearch.org
& Flowtown.com
http://www.flowtown.com/blog/whos-
using-twitter-and-how-theyre-using-it

Money By Images_of_Money
http://www.flickr.com/photos/59937401@
N07/5929474535/

Sheep by Donald Macleod
http://www.flickr.com/photos/
donaldmacleod/3439612846/
Complaint by Life As Art
http://www.flickr.com/photos/
lifeasart/271751746/

Directory by Si1very
http://www.flickr.com/photos/
silvery/1433791955/

Pleasesir by Sarah Jackson
http://www.flickr.com/photos/
traveljunkieoz/1001885444/

Viral by PNNL - Pacific Northwest National
Laboratory
http://www.flickr.com/photos/
pnnl/3636395128/

Ninja by Seth W.
http://www.flickr.com/photos/
sethw/381321976/

Language by Steve Webel
http://www.flickr.com/photos/
webel/65120154/

Crowd by Photos by Mavis
http://www.flickr.com/photos/portland_
mike/6140660504/

Spam by AJC1
http://www.flickr.com/photos/
ajc1/519906069/

Award Winner
The Library of Congress
http://www.flickr.com/photos/library_of_
congress/2179121608/

Concert crowd
Anirudh Koul
http://www.flickr.com/photos/
anirudhkoul/2632880868/

Free
Alan O'Rourke
http://www.flickr.com/photos/toddle_email_
newsletters/7002322316/in/photostream

Marketing Tactics Series

Other books from Alan O'Rourke. http://audiencestack.com/static/books.html

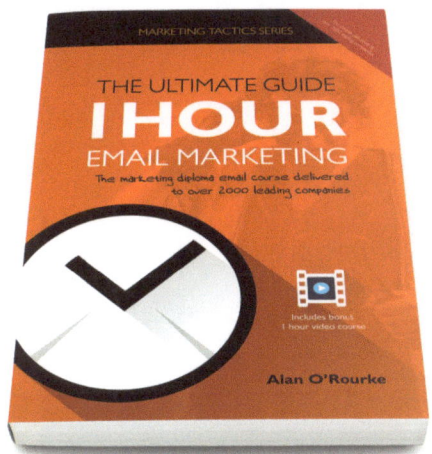

1 hour email marketing
The marketing diploma email course delivered to over 2000 leading companies.

30 days to sell
How the world's leading web sites convert trial users to paying customers.

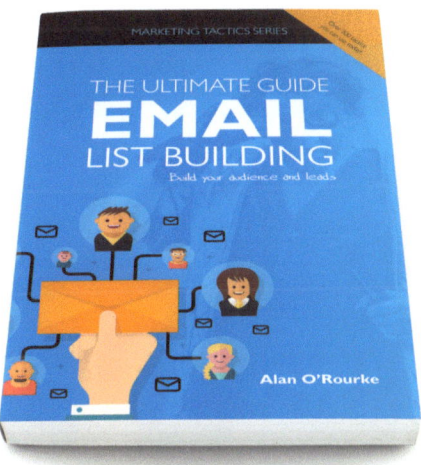

50 monster ideas to get more website links & customers
Tactics to get your website ranking and traffic a boost.

Email list building
Over 200 tactics from leading marketing and sales pros to build your audience and leads.

Thanks

A big thanks to the following people who continue to share their knowledge and experience for others to learn. Read and follow their blogs.

Rand Fishkin - Moz.com
Wil Reynolds - SeerInteractive.com
Martin MacDonald - Seoforums.com
Jane Copeland - Ayima Search Marketing
Russ Jones - Virante.com
The guys at Distilled.net
Alastair McDermott - websitedoctor.com
Paul Savage - emailtrainer.com
Paul Cawley - LearnInbound.com

50 Monster Ideas To get More Website Links   Customers

FREE SAMPLE

30

DAYS

TO SELL

Converting users from try to buy!

Proven automated sign-up campaigns
from the world's leading web companies

Alan O'Rourke

© Alan O'Rourke
All rights reserved. No part of this report may be reproduced or transmitted in any form or by any means,
electronic or mechanical, including photocopying, recording, faxing, emailing, posting online or by any information
storage and retrieval system, without written permission from the Publisher.
All emails and content copyright of the respective companies.
To purchase copies of other books by Alan, please visit http://audiencestack.com/static/books.html

Contents

Underpants Gnomes

One of the greatest business and marketing lessons from South Park, the animated Comedy Central show from Trey Stone and Matt Parker, is where a bunch of gnomes steal underpants from the townsfolk based on the following business model:
- Step 1. Collect underpants
- Step 2. -
- Step 3. Profit

while singing a Disney-like happy tune.

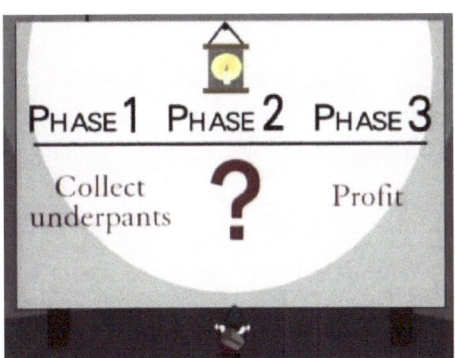 

When asked about step two, the gnomes stare blankly because obviously step three:profit is the important step.
See it here: http://beautiful-email-newsletters.com/underpants-gnomes/

Too many companies today work on exactly this model.
- Step 1. Collect sign ups
- Step 2. -
- Step 3. Profit

Then they look around confused when the profit does not materialise. Successful companies know that the selling starts after sign up. Step 2 needs to help, prompt and encourage users, while continuing to sell the benefits of the product or service, right up to the point users hand over their credit card; and in many cases beyond.

Collected here are the automated 30 day email campaigns of the world's leading web companies, picked apart and analysed to help you put together your own user activation campaigns.

Read on to see how these companies convert users from try to buy.

The perfect opening line

First impressions are important. Your first email sets the tone of your relationship and is a deciding factor on whether your subsequent emails, no matter how good, get read by your users.
The welcome email must walk the delicate line of getting a user to do enough to see the value of your business without asking too much and causing your email to be filed away for reading later (or never).

Compare the minimal, functional approach of Cliniko to bright and visual Asana who try get you excited about the next steps.

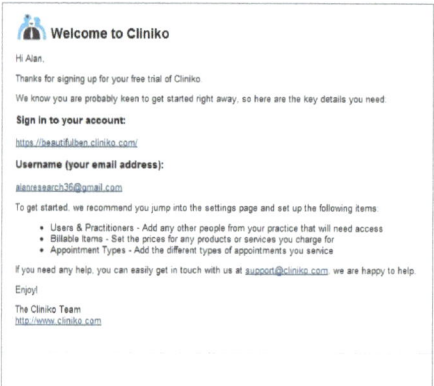
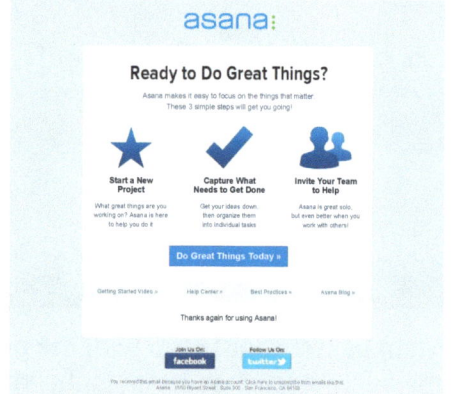

Bug tracking software Fogbugz.com tells you upfront what to expect over your trial to get you looking forward to their emails.

"Over the next six weeks I am going to send you exactly three emails. That's it. I just want to help you learn a bit more about FogBugz."

A welcome email most likely contains the users account information and will be referred to often. So a reminder to save the email with links to contact us, support and helpful guides like Squarespace.com is a good idea to help users.

Some companies like Mailchimp do two emails on sign up. One is your

Welcome to Squarespace

Your 14 day free trial starts today. Here is some important information about your new account. You should save this email, so you can refer to it later.

account information. A second separate welcome mail starts you on a series of 9 how-to guides of their key functionality.

It is very easy to forget how effective personal can be. Clinic booking site WhatClinic.com assign every new user a dedicated account manager so every mail comes from a real person, with a profile picture and signature. Likewise, e-commerce software Shopify.com (p.10) provide a user with their own guru to help. Print company Moo.com give their automated mails a personality called LittleMoo which gives a normal transactional email a sense of fun.

```
"Hello Alan
I'm Little MOO - the bit of software that will be
managing your order with moo.com. It will shortly be
sent to Big MOO, our print machine who will print it
for you in the next few days. I'll let you know when
it's done and on its way to you.
Thanks,
Little MOO, Print Robot"
```

30 days and counting...

You have 30 days to convert a user to a paying customer starting NOW. The clock is ticking. What will you do?

The following pages collect and analyse the messaging and strategy companies use to convert trial users to customers in the most important 30 days after sign-up. Each company's strategy is broken down and presented in an easy to understand, single page, visual guide.
You can dig into individual emails on subsequent pages to see how users are prompted to action.

While monthly email newsletters are not strictly part of an activation campaign you should be aware they will be going out at the same time so you need to ensure your messaging supports activation.

Read, analyze, and take note of what approach would work for your company and turn your users from try to buy.

Shopify

E-commerce software, online store builder 14-day trial

 From: Shopify <mailer@shopify.com>
Date: Thu, Mar 21, 2013 at 6:19 PM
Subject: Welcome to Shopify

01 day after sign-up

02

03

04

05

06

07

08

09

10

11

12

13 **From:** Shopify <mailer@shopify.com>
Date: Tue, Apr 2, 2013 at 9:27 AM
14 **Subject:** Your online store is about to close

15 **Monthly Newsletter**
From: Shopify Newsletter
<newsletter@shopify.com>
16
Date: Thu, Apr 4, 2013 at 10:18 PM
 From: Shopify <mailer@shopify.com>
Date: Thu, Apr 4, 2013 at 6:35 AM   **17** **Subject:** Get more online sales in April
Subject: Your online store has closed

18

19

20

21

22

23

24

25

26

27

28

29

30

31

Welcome to Shopify!

You've taken the first step towards world domination! Below you will find all of your account information, keep it in a safe place:

Your Store: http://beautifulben.myshopify.com/

Your store is currently password protected using the password "droosk". You can remove the password protection when you're ready to launch your store.

Your Store's Admin Area: http://beautifulben.myshopify.com/admin/

If you ever forget your password, you can always recover it by clicking here.

Get ready for some sales!

We've built a step-by-step tutorial into your Store Admin to get you started. You can do the tutorial steps in any order, or skip them completely, it's up to you.

Add Products

Customize Your Design

Add Content

Getting Paid

Setting Taxes

Shipping Settings

Domain Names

Meet your Shopify Guru!

We also provide every store owner with a personal Shopify Guru to help you make your store a success. Your Guru, Alex, can be reached via email at

alex.richards@shopify.com

Alex is available from Monday to Friday from 9am to 5pm EST.

The Shopify Guru Team

SUPPORT | FORUMS | THEME STORE | APP STORE | SHOPIFY EXPERTS | BLOG

© Shopify | 126 York Street, Ottawa, ON, K1N 5T5

Subject:
Welcome to Shopify

Sent:
Immediately

Call to action:
Get ready for some sales

Shopify have one of the nicer designed email sequences. It is great how they introduce your personal account manager Alex and devote a full third of the email to it. They sell the benefits along with the next steps they want you to take.

Your store is about to close!

Hey beautifulben,

Your free Shopify trial will expire in less than 2 days! If you don't want your online store to be closed, please log in and pick a plan. If you have forgotten your password, you can easily recover it here.

Which Plan is Best for You?

Our friendly Sales Team would be happy to help you find the perfect plan for beautifulben. You can reach them by phone (1-888-SHOPIFY) or use our Sales Contact Form.

Get $100 in Credits Today

Pick a plan today and we'll give $100 in free credit for Google AdWords. You can use this to get customers to your online store.

Need Some Help?

Your Shopify Guru, Alex, is standing by to help you get your site up and running and an be reached via email at:

alex.richards@shopify.com

Alex is available from Monday to Friday from 9am to 5pm EST.

The Shopify Guru Team

SUPPORT   FORUMS   THEME STORE   APP STORE   SHOPIFY EXPERTS   BLOG

© Shopify   126 York Street, Ottawa, ON, K1N 5T5

 13

Subject:
Your online store is about to close

Sent:
Twelve days after signup.

Call to action:
Buy today
& get $100 google adwords credits.

Again Shopify reinforce the personal touch. You can phone and chat about what plan you should buy. Shopify know the power of real people.

Your store has closed :(

 15

Hey beautifulben,

Uh-oh. Your free trial of Shopify has ended and your store is now closed.

Don't worry, nothing has been lost and you can easily re-open your store by picking a plan and entering your payment details.

All of us at Shopify are dedicated to building the best ecommerce platform possible and we hope you enjoyed your trial. Should you have any questions or feedback don't hesitate to get in touch with us by phone (1-888-SHOPIFY) or using our contact form.

Thank you,
The Shopify Team

SUPPORT | FORUMS | THEME STORE | APP STORE | SHOPIFY EXPERTS | BLOG

© Shopify | 126 York Street, Ottawa, ON, K1N 5T5

Subject:
Your online store has closed

Sent:
Fourteen days after signup

Call to action:
Re-open your store by picking a plan

I like the extra hook of saying they have not yet deleted your data. The fear of losing something is a much more powerful driver of behaviour than the want to get something.

15

shopify

Start selling more in April

Dear Alan O'Rourke,

Learning how to launch and grow your online store *can* be challenging. But it doesn't have to be! This month we're excited to announce the launch of Ecommerce University – a free resource to help you grow your business. We'll also tell you about our increased support coverage, pass on some great advice from our forums, and share two of this month's most popular themes.

Learn how to sell more online

Our freshly launched Ecommerce University is a collection of advice on how to sell online. You'll find ebooks, articles, videos, and discussion forums full of tips and tricks for beginners to experts alike – and it's all free.

Check out the new Ecommerce University.

Ecommerce
University

Talk to us for free 24x7

We've expanded our customer service capacity to make sure you have the support you need, whenever you need it. Shopify gurus are always available to take your call or answer your email 24 hours a day, 7 days a week.

We also have toll-free and local phone numbers for:

UK: 0800 808 5233
Australia: 03 8400 4750
New Zealand: 07 788 6026
North America: 1 888 746 7439

The best of the forum

Our discussion forums are a place where you can ask questions and connect with other store owners. Here are some of this month's best conversations:

- How to price plus sized clothes
- Opinions on product prices
- Do I need a photographer?
- How do you get rid of old inventory?
- How to verify your Shopify website on Pinterest
- TV advertising: does anyone do it?
- Best tips for social media marketing

The best of the Shopify Blog

Our blog is filled with articles to help you build your business and sell more. Here are some of the most popular blog posts from the past month:

- New Shopify Apps to Help You Sell More
- 10 Must Know Image Optimization Tips
- All About US Trademarks
- Best of the Build-A-Business Mentor Tips

Monthly Newsletter

Subject:
Get more online sales in April

Sent:
Fourteen days after signup

Content
Business & marketing advice
Sell more in April
Learning resources
Free 24x7 support
Join our community
Our best blog posts
Try our theme store

Cliniko
Medical Practice Management Software 30-day trial

 From: Cliniko <support@cliniko.com>
Date: Tue, Mar 26, 2013 at 4:24 PM
Subject: Welcome to Cliniko!

 01

02

03

 04   **From:** Jim Sadusky <support@cliniko.com>
Date: Fri, Mar 29, 2013 at 4:30 PM
05   **Subject:** Need help with Cliniko?

06

07

08

09

10

11

12

13

14

15

16

17

18

19

20

21

 22   **Monthly Newsletter**
From: Cliniko <info@cliniko.com>
23   **Date:** Tue, Apr 16, 2013 at 6:28 AM
Subject: Cliniko News - April 2013

 **From:** Cliniko <support@cliniko.com>
Date: Thu, Apr 18, 2013 at 5:36 PM
Subject: Cliniko - 7 days of free trial left

24

25

26

27

28

29

30

 31   **From:** support@cliniko.com
Date: Thu, Apr 25, 2013 at 5:43 PM
Subject: Cliniko subscription ended

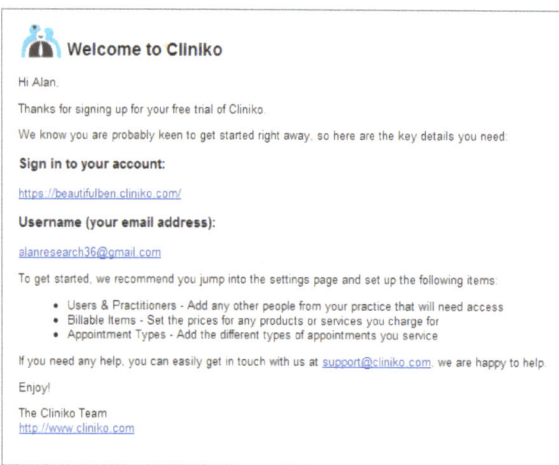

Subject:
Welcome to Cliniko!

Sent:
Immediately

Call to action
Set up your clinic

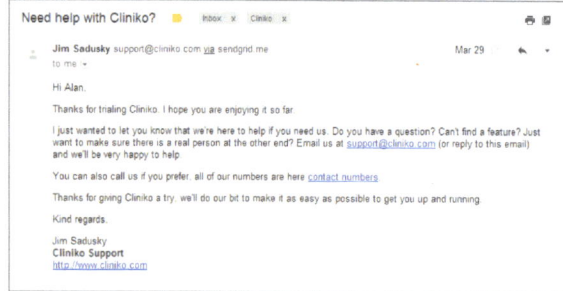

Subject:
Need help with Cliniko?

Sent:
Three days after signup

Call to action:
Contact us. We are real & here to help.

 The personal touch from Jim helps this email seem genuine and helpful.

Cliniko News. All the latest changes and information.

Cliniko News - April 2013

Hi Everyone,

It's time for another update!

Firstly, we've had Matt Jones join our team a few weeks ago. Matt is a devops and will be spending his time making sure Cliniko is reliable and fast. He has some big plans for infrastructure improvements and we'll announce more as we get closer. Matt's addition brings the Cliniko team up to 8 now. You can read a bit more about Matt here http://www.cliniko.com/blog/256/matt-has-joined-the-cliniko-team/.

We've also been really hard at work on developing new features and improving existing ones. Further below you'll see a list of the main changes we've released in the last couple of months, but really it's nothing compared to what's coming. These are the big 3 that we are currently working on (click the links to see the previews):

- Letter Writing - https://support.cliniko.com/entries/20182502-Letters-to-patients
- Xero Integration - https://support.cliniko.com/entries/20245331-Integration-with-accounting-packages
- iCal Integration - https://support.cliniko.com/entries/20236242-iCal-integration

We are getting much closer on all of those and can't wait to release them.

On top of all the changes coming out, we also have many new businesses signing up to use Cliniko every day. There have now been over 2 million appointments created in Cliniko and over 1 million patients. We are humbled and thankful for everyones support and it motivates us even further to keep delivering for you all.

Thanks!

Joel Friedlaender
Founder - Cliniko

Recent Changes

Practitioners can view their own revenue reports (01-March-2013)

We made a change so that practitioners can access the practitioner revenue reports, for themselves only.

Contacts (09-March-2013)

We added **Contacts** into Cliniko. This is used to store the details of anyone that isn't a patient. This could be used for other practitioners, suppliers, insurers or anyone else really.

Stay up to date

Subscribe here:
Cliniko updates and changes

Like our facebook page:
Cliniko facebook page

Follow us on twitter:
@cliniko

Changes to treatment note autosaving (14-March-2013)

We made a change to treatment note autosaving. This was to allow it to work even if your internet dropped out and a few other benefits too. This change has however been met with mixed reviews, you can see the details and discussion here https://support.cliniko.com/entries/21650900-Big-improvements-to-treatment-note-autosaving. We have more improvements planned for this change.

Security updates (19-March-2013)

We released a few security updates to ensure our security stays top notch and is up to date with current threats.

Improvements to data importing (04-April-2013)

We made some big improvements to data imports. It no longer struggles with large import files and it also lets you "undo" your data imports within 48 hours of importing. You can see your historical imports too.

22

Monthly newsletter

Subject:
Cliniko News - April 2013

Sent:
Twenty one days after signup.

Content:
Letter from the founder
New staff (we are growing)
System updates & new features

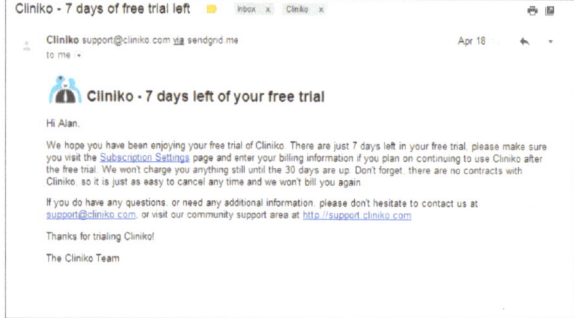

Subject:
Cliniko - 7 days of free trial left

Sent:
Twenty three days after signup.

Call to action:
Add your credit card for uninterrupted service.

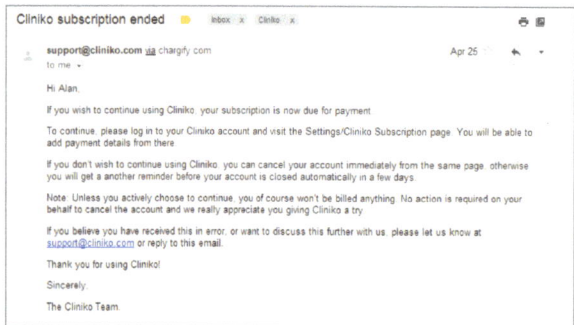

Subject:
Cliniko subscription ended

Sent:
Thirty days after signup.

Call to action:
**Times up.
To continue, log in and add payment details.**

 A great series of mails but Cliniko undermine the message and power of this mail. They say time is up and pay now. Then say, oh hang on, you still have a few days. I am lazy so I will hang on for a few more days.

It's common to follow up after a few days with a last, last chance mail or even a special offer. A hail mary email it is called. But best not to warn users it is coming.

Order 30 Days To Sell

"So many books on marketing focus on customer acquisition. This book however focuses on customer *activation* as the necessary precursor before any customer will part with their cash for your products. This book is purely focused on practical examples of useful stuff you can put into action in just about any business using email to market to customers. - Eoghan C. Jennings, Startup Bootcamp.
http://audiencestack.com/static/books.html

Available in paperback and digital

www.ingramcontent.com/pod-product-compliance
Lightning Source LLC
Chambersburg PA
CBHW041111180526
45172CB00001B/206